INSPIRATIONAL LIVES

JESSICA ENNIS

CHAMPION ATHLETE

Simon Hart

WAYLAND

First published in 2013 by Wayland

Wayland
338 Euston Road
London NW1 3BH

Wayland Australia
Level 17/207 Kent Street
Sydney, NSW 2000

Editor: Nicola Edwards
Design: Basement68

A catalogue record for this book is
available from the British Library.

ISBN: 978 0 7502 7998 7

Printed in China

Wayland is a division of
Hachette Children's Books,
an Hachette UK company.

www.hachette.co.uk

Picture acknowledgements:
The author and publisher would like
to thank the following for allowing
their pictures to be reproduced in this
publication:
Cover: Owen Humphreys/PA Wire; p4
Paul Gilham/Getty Images; p5 David
Davies/PA Wire; p6 Dave Thompson/PA
Wire; p7 Jonathan Pow/PA Wire; p8 Getty
Images; p9 Michael Steele/Getty Images;
p10 Gareth Copley/PA; p11 AP Photo/
Thomas Kienzle; p12 AP Photo/Winfried
Rothermel; p13 Getty Images/Getty
Images for Aviva; p14 Bill Frakes /Sports
Illustrated/Getty Images; p15 AP Photo/
Matt Dunham; p16 Osama Faisal/AP/
Press Association Images; p17 AP Photo/
Matt Dunham; p18 John Stillwell/PA Wire;
p19 Adam Davy/EMPICS Sport; p20 John
Giles/PA Wire; p21 Dave Higgens/PA Wire;
p22 Ben Curtis/AP/Press Association
Images; p23 Dave Thompson/PA Wire;
p24 Anna Gowthorpe/PA Wire; p25 David
Davies/PA Wire; p26 John Giles/
PA Wire; p27 John Giles/PA Wire; p28
Anna Gowthorpe/PA Wire; p29 David
Davies/PA Wire

Contents

The world's greatest all-rounder

At the 2012 Olympics, Jessica Ennis proved herself to be the greatest all-round female athlete in the world. She won a gold medal in the **heptathlon** – the ultimate test of an athlete's speed, **endurance** and strength. Not only that, she triumphed by the second largest winning margin in Olympic history.

The heptathlon is one of the toughest events in athletics. Competition takes place over two exhausting days and consists of seven different disciplines. Points are awarded in each event and to be a champion, you have to excel in all seven. At London 2012, Jessica did exactly that.

A golden moment for Jessica as she crosses the finish line in the 800 metres to be crowned Olympic heptathlon champion in London.

Jessica's victory was all the more remarkable because of what happened to her four years earlier. A few months before she was due to compete at the 2008 Olympics in Beijing, China, she suffered three **fractures** in her right foot. Doctors told her that the injury was so serious that she might have to give up being an athlete.

Jessica was heartbroken at the news but refused to give up. Even before her foot had healed properly, she began training again in the gym. Her amazing fighting spirit paid off when she returned to competition in 2009. At the World Championships in Berlin, she stunned her rivals by winning the gold medal.

The following year, Jessica also won the European title, but it was an Olympic gold medal that she wanted to make up for her disappointment in 2008. On August 4, 2012, in front of an ecstatic London crowd, Jessica fulfilled her dream.

INSPIRATION

"I think the Olympics and Paralympics have brought so many amazing women to the forefront of people's minds and inspired so many young girls around the country." – Jessica Ennis.

A beaming Jessica shows her Olympic gold medal to the thousands of fans who lined the streets of London for the athletes' victory parade.

Early potential

Jessica Ennis was born in Sheffield, Yorkshire, on January 28, 1986. She still lives in the city. Although money was tight when Jessica was growing up, she enjoyed a happy childhood with her parents, Vinnie and Alison, and her sister, Carmel, who is three years younger than her.

One of the first things Jessica learned from her parents was the importance of hard work. Vinnie, who was born in Jamaica and moved to Britain when he was 12, is a painter and decorator, while Alison is a social worker. When Jessica was young, Alison used to work night shifts while Vinnie looked after the two girls.

Jessica attended Sharrow Junior School and, from the age of 11, King Ecgbert Secondary School. When she was 10, her mother spotted an advert for a summer camp in Sheffield offering children the chance to try out various athletics events. Jessica went along and loved every minute of it. She also impressed the **coaches** so much that she was awarded her first athletics prize: a pair of trainers.

Among Jessica's biggest fans are her mother Alison (left), sister Carmel and father Vinnie.

WOW!

Jessica was bullied as a young girl because she was so small. Later, when she became successful at athletics, the same bullies wanted to be her friends.

At the invitation of one of the coaches, Jessica started training once a week at the Don Valley Stadium in Sheffield. Most of the time she practised sprinting but she was also keen on the hurdles and high jump. Despite being very small for her age, she was so good at the high jump that she could leap higher than many older boys at her school.

When Jessica was 12 she joined City of Sheffield Athletics Club. A year later, she started training with a coach at the club called Toni Minichiello, who had a reputation for being a very hard task-master. Toni ended up coaching Jessica throughout her athletics career.

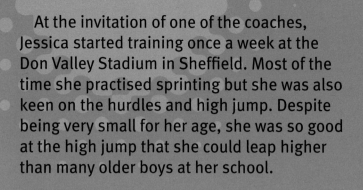

WOW!

Jessica was named 'Sportswoman Of The Year' by her school at the age of 14.

During the 2012 Olympics, fans gathered to watch Jessica's performance on giant TV screens at the Don Valley Stadium in Sheffield, where her career as an athlete began.

A growing medal collection

Jessica made rapid progress and in 2000, aged 14, she won her first gold medal, finishing first in the junior girls' high jump competition at the English Schools Championships. Her winning leap of 1.70 metres was well above her own height.

Because Jessica was so talented at other athletics events, her coach, Toni Minichiello, decided to enter her in 'combined events' competitions such as the five-event **pentathlon** and the seven-event heptathlon. In 2001, she won the silver medal in the English Schools pentathlon and, a year later, silver in the English Schools heptathlon.

By now, Jessica was dreaming of a career as an athlete. She was training every night and competing at weekends, which meant she had to make sacrifices in her life. While her friends went on nights out, Jessica often had to stay at home.

INSPIRATION

Jessica's former teacher, Chris Eccles, says Jessica has become a **role model** for pupils at King Ecgbert School. "They are inspired by her because they can see someone from their own town being so successful," he says.

Toni Minichiello (left) has been Jessica's coach since she was 13 years old. She says he is like a second father to her.

Jessica's dedication was rewarded when, aged 16, she was picked to represent Great Britain in an international match in Switzerland, and finished second in the heptathlon. A year later, in 2003, she took part in what was then the biggest event of her career when she was selected in the heptathlon for the World Youth Championships in Sherbrooke, Canada. Against the world's best young athletes, she finished a very encouraging fifth.

When she was 18, Jessica began a **psychology** degree at Sheffield University, though the amount of hours she was devoting to athletics made it quite difficult to find time to study. Meanwhile, she was getting stronger and stronger as a heptathlete. In July 2005, she celebrated her first international title when she won gold at the European Junior Championships in Kaunas, Lithuania.

TOP TIP

Jessica says it is important to try a variety of sports when you are young. "You've just got to go out and enjoy your sport," she says. "There is time later on to focus on one discipline."

Jessica competes in the 100 metres hurdles during the World Youth Championships in Sherbrooke, Canada, in 2003.

Senior breakthrough

Having excelled at junior level, it was time for Jessica to test herself against adult athletes. Her opportunity came in 2006 when she was selected to compete for England at the Commonwealth Games in Melbourne, Australia. It was an exciting new experience for Jessica. There were huge crowds inside the stadium and the world's **media** watching her every step of the way.

Although it was Jessica's first major senior championship, she was far from **overawed**. By the end of the two days of heptathlon competition she had a total score of 6,269 points, more than 300 points higher than her previous best total. Jessica's score was enough to earn her the bronze medal, with gold going to her England team-mate, Kelly Sotherton.

Jessica (centre) is narrowly beaten by England team-mate Kelly Sotherton in the 200 metres at the 2006 Commonwealth Games in Melbourne, Australia.

WOW!

Kelly Sotherton called Jessica 'Tadpole' because she was so small. Jessica was not keen on the nickname!

The result showed Jessica was now ready to compete at senior level, though there was still a long way to go to beat the world's best. At the European Championships in Gothenburg, Sweden, later in the year, Jessica set a new **personal best** of 6,287 points but it was only good enough for eighth place because the standard of her opponents was so high.

In 2007, Jessica had another chance to compete against the top athletes in her sport when she was selected for her first senior World Championships in Osaka, Japan. This time, Jessica produced a performance that left many of her rivals talking about her as a future champion.

Still aged only 21, she improved her personal best again to 6,469 points to finish in fourth place. Although she narrowly missed out on a bronze medal, Jessica was delighted to have pushed her opponents so close.

*The **shot put** requires a lot of upper body strength. Here Jessica competes at the 2007 World Championships in Osaka, Japan.*

TOP TIP

"Doing the same training day in day will not make any progress towards your intended goal. Regular yet different training and exercise is important." – Jessica Ennis's coach, Toni Minichiello

Injury nightmare

It was 2008, the year of the Beijing Olympics, and Jessica was improving so rapidly that she was being talked about as a possible gold medallist. Her chances had increased after Sweden's Carolina Kluft, the defending Olympic champion and world record-holder, had recently announced her retirement from the heptathlon.

Three months before the start of the Olympics, Jessica and most of her main rivals gathered in the Austrian town of Götzis for a warm-up heptathlon. Jessica was feeling fit and eager to build on her excellent result in Osaka. But then disaster struck.

WOW!

Jessica has said that she was so upset after her foot injury that she cried for about seven days.

Jessica had been feeling a slight ache in her right foot throughout the first day of competition. After her 200 metres race, the last event of day one, her foot was so painful that she had no choice but to pull out of the heptathlon. The following morning she flew to London for a scan to find out was causing the problem.

Jessica clears the bar in the high jump in Götzis, Austria, in 2008, but just hours later she was hobbling with a serious foot injury.

The doctors had terrible news. They told Jessica that she had three serious stress fractures in her foot. Competing in Beijing was out of the question, they said. Even worse, they told her that there was a chance her career as a world-class athlete might be over at the age of 22.

Jessica was devastated. Missing the Olympics was one thing but the thought of giving up the sport she loved was too much to bear. Jessica was determined to carry on. Even though she was on crutches and unable to stand on her injured foot, she began to do some weights exercises in the gym. The fight-back had begun.

WOW!

Jessica's parents had already paid for flights and hotels for the Beijing Olympics before Jessica was injured. They lost thousands of pounds when she had to pull out of the Games.

After recovering from her injury, Jessica is back in training at a British warm-weather camp in Portugal in 2009.

On top of the world

After a winter of hard work in the gym, Jessica received the news she had been hoping for. A scan showed that her injured foot had healed and she was clear to compete again. The doctors' fears that she might have to give up her athletics career proved **unfounded**.

In May, 2009, Jessica travelled to Desenzano in northern Italy for her first heptathlon since fracturing her foot. She was nervous, but she need not have worried. Incredibly, she produced her best ever display of running, jumping and throwing with a personal best score of 6,587 points. The next best athlete was more than 500 points behind.

Jessica's performance meant she was ranked No 1 in the world when she went to Berlin, Germany, later that summer to compete at the World Championships. It was the perfect chance to make up for her disappointment of missing the Beijing Olympics the previous year.

WOW!

Jessica equalled the British high jump record in Desenzano with a massive leap of 1.95 metres. Amazingly, it was 30cm higher than Jessica's own height.

An aerial view of Jessica competing in the long jump during the 2009 World Championships in Berlin, Germany.

Among Jessica's opponents in Berlin was Ukrainian athlete Nataliya Dobrynska, who won the heptathlon gold medal in Beijing, as well as Russian Tatyana Chernova, who won the Olympic bronze.

In the famous stadium where the Olympics were held in 1936, Jessica was simply outstanding. She led the competition from start to finish, ending up with her best ever score of 6,731 points. It was 238 points higher than the second-placed athlete, Germany's Jennifer Oeser. Dobrynska finished in fourth place.

Jessica may have missed the Olympics but she was now the world champion. After the misery of her foot injury, she was now the best all-round athlete on the planet.

Jessica shows her incredible all-round ability as she prepares to throw the *javelin* at the World Championships in Berlin in 2009.

INSPIRATION

Jessica says missing out on the Beijing Olympics made her a better and stronger athlete. When her body ached in training, she remembered how much worse she felt when she was injured.

A winning habit

Jessica's victory in Berlin turned her into one of Britain's most popular sportswomen. The public loved how she had fought back from injury to win a world gold medal – and her winning streak had only just begun.

In March, 2010, Jessica won her second world title in the space of six months. At the World Indoor Championships in Doha, Qatar, she triumphed in the pentathlon. Nataliya Dobrynska was Jessica's closest rival but proved no match for the British athlete. Jessica won by 86 points with a score of 4,937. It was the highest total in the history of the championships.

Two months later, Jessica returned to Götzis for the first time since she injured her foot there in 2008. She was very apprehensive because of all the bad memories, but this time it was a much happier occasion. Despite torrential rain, Jessica was a comfortable winner.

A proud moment for Jessica as she shows off her gold medal at the 2010 World Championships. Nataliya Dobrynska (left) of Ukraine won the silver and Russia's Tatyana Chernova (right) won the bronze.

As a reward for her good **form**, Jessica was made captain of the British team for the European Championships in Barcelona, Spain, later that summer. When it came to the heptathlon, once again it was Dobrynska who provided the strongest challenge to Jessica, and the competition turned out to be very close. Jessica eventually won the gold medal, but only by a narrow 45-point margin.

Jessica had now won two world titles and one European gold medal in the space of a year. She was so successful that people began to describe her as the 'queen of combined events'. By the end of 2010, life became even happier for Jessica when she announced her engagement to her boyfriend, Andy Hill, though the wedding would have to wait until after the 2012 London Olympics.

Jessica celebrates another amazing victory, this time at the European Championships in Barcelona in 2010.

WOW!

Jessica could not complete the lap of honour after her triumph in Berlin because the men's 100 metres final was taking place. Instead, she sat down by the track and watched Usain Bolt break the world record.

Joy turns to anxiety

Jessica's winning streak continued in 2011 when, in May, she returned to Göztis, Austria, and defeated all of her heptathlon rivals again. To add to her delight, her success as an athlete was rewarded with an honour from the Queen when she was appointed an MBE (Member of the British Empire).

Since her comeback from injury in 2009, Jessica had been unbeaten in all heptathlon and pentathlon competitions. It was as if she was **invincible**. Her next big event of the summer was the World Championships in Daegu, South Korea, and everyone expected her to win another gold medal.

Jessica shows off her MBE at Buckingham Palace, accompanied by her fiancé, Andy Hill (left) and her parents, Alison and Vinnie.

WOW!

A waxwork figure of Jessica was unveiled at Madame Tussauds in London in 2011. It took four months to make and cost £150,000.

Unfortunately for Jessica, things did not go exactly to plan. In a very close contest, Russian athlete Tatyana Chernova produced the best performance of her life to put Jessica under a lot of pressure. On the second day of the heptathlon, Jessica needed to throw the javelin about 45 metres to stay level with Chernova but she could manage only 39.95 metres. That was way below Jessica's usual standard and her failure meant Chernova won the gold. Jessica had to make do with the silver medal.

Although she tried to hide her disappointment, Jessica was very upset her by her defeat. She had become so used to winning gold medals that receiving the silver felt like a let-down.

There was now just one year to go until the London Olympics and Jessica's experience in Daegu was a warning of how tough the competition would be. Jessica knew she had to work even harder in training to fulfil her dream of becoming an Olympic champion.

INSPIRATION

Jessica says seeing a photograph of Tatyana Chernova celebrating her victory at the World Championships made her even more determined to succeed because she never wanted to be second best again.

After her run of victories, Jessica is disappointed to be beaten by Tatyana Chernova (right) at the 2011 World Championships in Daegu, South Korea.

Back on track

Jessica was in great form during the 2012 indoor season, setting a personal best for the 60 metres hurdles, but she was not the only athlete in excellent physical shape. At the World Indoor Championships in Turkey, Jessica again had to settle for the silver medal after Ukrainian Nataliya Dobrynska set a pentathlon world record to win the gold.

After her defeat in Daegu the previous summer, Jessica had now lost two multi-event competitions in a row. It was hardly the best preparation for the Olympics. She badly needed to get back to winning ways.

Jessica did not have to wait long. In May, the world's leading heptathletes, including Chernova and Dobrynska, gathered in Götzis, Austria, for the final warm-up competition before the London Olympics. This time there was no stopping Jessica. In what turned out to be a perfect Olympic rehearsal, Jessica won with a huge total of 6,906 points. It was the highest total of her career and broke the British heptathlon record.

Jessica celebrates her record-breaking performance in Götzis, Austria, in 2012.

WOW!

Jessica became only the eighth woman in history to score 6,900 points or more in a heptathlon. She was the first British athlete to do so.

20

She was also becoming known as the 'Face of the Games'. Posters and photographs of Jessica were popping up everywhere and she also appeared in several TV adverts.

Jessica was now one of the most famous athletes in the British Olympic team but she was determined not to get carried away with her high profile. There was still the small matter of an Olympic title to win.

The Olympics were now only two months away, and Jessica's brilliant performance in Götzis meant that she was now the firm favourite to win the gold medal in London.

WOW!

Before the London Olympics, a giant picture of Jessica was painted in a field on the flight path to London's Heathrow Airport so that people arriving for the Games could see her image.

Golden girl

On August 3rd, 2012, Jessica's big day arrived. It was the first morning of the two-day Olympic heptathlon competition and 80,000 fans were packed inside the Olympic stadium in London to watch the first event: the 100 metres hurdles. They were not disappointed. In an amazing race, Jessica triumphed in an outstanding time of 12.54 seconds. It was a United Kingdom hurdles record and equalled the winning time in the hurdles at the 2008 Beijing Olympics. What a start!

After the high jump and the shot put, the last event of the first day was the 200 metres, and once again Jessica produced a lifetime best performance with a superb time of 22.83 seconds. It meant that after four of the seven events, Jessica was leading the Olympic competition by 184 points.

WOW!

Jessica's winning time of 12.54 seconds in the 100 metres hurdles was the fastest hurdles time ever recorded during a heptathlon competition.

Jessica makes the perfect start to her Olympic heptathlon competition when she breaks the UK record for the 100 m hurdles.

The second day went just as well. The long jump has never been one of Jessica's strongest events but an excellent leap of 6.48 metres kept her well in the lead. Then came the javelin, and Jessica once again showed her fantastic form with a throw of 47.49 metres. It was the longest javelin throw of her life and meant that the gold medal was almost hers with just one event remaining.

The final event was the 800 metres. Jessica had such a big points **advantage** that she did not need to win the race but she was eager to put on a show. As she crossed the finish line in first place, she raised her arms in celebration. She had finally achieved her dream of winning an Olympic gold medal.

HONOURS BOARD

Olympic Games heptathlon result

Gold: Jessica Ennis (GB) 6,955 points (British record)

Silver: Lilli Schwarzkopf (Germany) 6,649 points

Bronze: Tatyana Chernova (Russia) 6,628 points.

Breakdown of Jessica's seven events:
100 metres hurdles: 12.54 seconds* (1,195 points)
High jump: 1.86 metres (1,054 points)
Shot put: 14.28m (813 points)
200 metres: 22.83 seconds (1,096 points)
Long jump: 6.48 metres (1,001 points)
Javelin: 47.49 metres (812 points)
800 metres: 2 minutes, 8.65 seconds (984 points).

*Jessica's time was a UK record for the 100 metres hurdles.

During Jessica's medal presentation ceremony, she shed tears of joy. Her emotion showed how much her gold medal meant to her.

Honouring a champion

The London Olympics came to a close on August 12th, 2012, but Jessica's celebrations went on a lot longer. They began with an open-top bus parade through central London with the rest of her British Olympic and Paralympic team-mates. Afterwards, Jessica and her fellow athletes were invited to Buckingham Palace for a reception with the Queen.

Thousands of fans lined the streets of London for the parade, and thousands more braved the heavy rain to pay tribute to Jessica when she returned home to Sheffield for a celebration in the city centre. The City Council rewarded her with a special honour called the 'Freedom of the City'.

INSPIRATION

"Even when it comes to the smallest things, Jessica's competitive nature just takes over. We could be throwing stuff in a bin from five metres away and yet she has still got to win. That's just her, and that's why she is now an Olympic champion." – Jessica's coach, Toni Minichiello.

A glorious homecoming as thousands of people turn out in Sheffield to honour Jessica's gold-medal-winning achievement.

At the end of the year, Jessica's golden achievement was recognised by the Queen when she was appointed a CBE (Commander of the British Empire). The British public also honoured her by voting her into second place behind cyclist Bradley Wiggins at the BBC Sports Personality of the Year awards.

Jessica returned to training about six weeks after the Olympics. Despite her many celebrity appearances, she needed to stay fit to prepare for the 2013 season.

But, apart from athletics, Jessica had something else on her mind. She and her fiancé, Andy Hill, had been engaged since 2010 but Jessica's preparations for the London Olympics meant there had been no time to get married. With the Olympics now over, she and Andy finally had the chance to organise their wedding.

HONOURS BOARD
All-time British heptathlon rankings

1. Jessica Ennis 6,955 points (2012)
2. Denise Lewis 6,831 points (2000)
3. Judy Simpson 6,623 points (1986)
4. Kelly Sotherton 6,547 points (2005)
5. Katarina Johnson-Thompson 6,267 points (2012)

Jessica Ennis and her fiancé, Andy Hill, in the audience at the BBC Sports Personality of the Year Awards in December, 2012.

A day in the life of Jessica Ennis

Jessica has seven events to practise, which means her training schedule has to be very organised. Instead of practising all seven on the same day, Jessica prefers to concentrate on one or two events in each training session. On one day of the week, for example, she practises her long jump. On another day, she turns her attention to the hurdles and high jump.

Most of Jessica's training sessions take place in Sheffield, where she first took up athletics. She trains six days a week, with one rest day. Even her day off can be busy because she often has to do some work for one of her **sponsors**, such as a photo shoot or interviews with newspapers and broadcasters.

WOW!

Jessica has been showered with sponsorship offers from leading companies. She has signed deals to promote Adidas, Olay, Aviva, BP, Omega, Jaguar, Powerade and British Airways.

Jessica meets the press as she protects her muscles in a wheely bin of icy water.

On a typical training day, Jessica spends the morning practising her hurdles with her coach, Toni Minichiello. After lunch, she works on her shot put. Then it is time for some **plyometrics**, which are exercises such as leaping over hurdles or onto boxes to make her muscles more powerful. Jessica's day will finish with some weight-lifting in the gym.

As well as Toni, Jessica has a team of experts around her to help her get into the best physical shape. They include a **physiotherapist** and a **soft-tissue therapist** to treat any injuries and prevent any pains and niggles from becoming more serious. She also has a separate javelin coach and a **biomechanist,** who films her during her training sessions to make sure her technique is as effective as possible. Jessica calls her group of helpers 'Team Jennis'.

WOW!

Jessica is a big chocolate-lover. Because she burns off so many calories in training, she allows herself a chocolate treat every day.

Jessica's achievements as an athlete have made her famous all over the world. Here, while training for a competition in Götzis, Austria, she runs past a huge poster of herself being used to advertise the event.

27

The impact of Jessica Ennis

As Jessica celebrated her gold medal at the London Olympics, it was easy to forget how sad she'd felt four years earlier. After suffering a serious foot injury in 2008, doctors warned that her athletics career might be over. Her Olympic victory showed what a true fighter she is. She never gave up on her dream. The injury just made her even more determined.

Jessica's achievements at World and European Championships and at the Olympic Games have made her one of the most famous sportswomen in the world. They have also made her an important role model for young girls.

INSPIRATION

After her Olympic triumph, Jessica became a 'Living for Sport' ambassador to help improve the lives of thousands of young people in secondary schools across the UK.

Jessica has become a role model for aspiring young athletes such as these teenagers in Sheffield.

In Britain, women's sport does not get as much media coverage as men's sport. Also, while many young boys dream of becoming footballers, rugby players or cricketers, a lot of girls drop out of sport when they are teenagers, thinking that being sporty is not feminine.

Jessica has shown that being a top sportswoman can also be very glamorous. During the London Olympics, she was the 'Face of the Games' as posters of her appeared all over the country. After winning the gold, she was in demand for photo-shoots and TV appearances. She was more like a film-star than an athlete.

Part of Jessica's appeal to young girls is that she is such a down-to-earth person. She remains modest about her achievements and proud of her ordinary background in Sheffield. Hopefully, her story will inspire many others to take up sport and perhaps one day even win an Olympic gold medal.

The Duchess of Cambridge chats to Jessica backstage at the 2012 BBC Sports Personality of the Year Awards.

INSPIRATION

"A lot of hard work went into winning that gold medal and I hope I have inspired people to not only continue in sport but seek new challenges." – Jessica Ennis

Have you got what it takes to be an Olympic champion?

1) When you are taking part in sport or playing a video or board game, how important is it for you to win?
a) Really important. I just cannot bear losing.
b) Quite important. Winning is always enjoyable but you have to lose sometimes.
c) Not important at all. I'm not a very competitive person.

2) Do you enjoy running around and being active?
a) I love it. I always feel that I have a lot of energy to burn off.
b) Sometimes, if I'm in the mood.
c) Not really. I'd much rather do another activity.

3) Could you commit yourself to regular training sessions after school and at weekends?
a) Absolutely. Doing exercise is a fun way to spend your spare time.
b) I could manage some training sessions but I wouldn't want to give up all of my relaxation time.
c) No way. My free time is far too valuable.

4) How do you react if you can't do something such as a puzzle or a video game?
a) I just try even harder until I can do it.
b) I have a few attempts but if I still can't manage it, I give up.
c) I give up straight away. I don't like wasting my time on something I can't do.

5) What would you do if you got injured and couldn't train?
a) Ask my teacher or coach to suggest some training exercises I could do without making the injury worse.
b) Wait until I am completely healed and then start training again.
c) I'd put my feet up and eat whatever I want.

6) Would you be prepared to give up your favourite foods and stick to a healthy diet?
a) Yes. Eating the right foods is so important if you want to be good at sport.
b) I'd do my best but some foods would be impossible to give up.
c) I eat what I like and I won't change my diet.

7) Do you get nervous before taking part in sport?
a) Yes, nervous and excited. I'm just so anxious to do my best.
b) Yes, I get very nervous. I'm so worried about being a failure.
c) No, never. After all, it's only a game.

RESULTS

Mostly As: You have just the right, competitive attitude to be a champion. Now it's up to you to prove it on the sports field.

Mostly Bs: You have a pretty positive outlook but becoming a champion requires a lot of dedication and hard work. Begin by staying fit and active and see how things develop.

Mostly Cs: You don't seem cut out to be an Olympic champion but it would a shame to turn your back on sport altogether. It's an enjoyable way to stay fit and healthy.

Glossary

advantage A position of superiority over someone else.

biomechanist Someone who studies the science of how a living body moves.

coaches Training or fitness advisors.

endurance The ability to train or work for a long period of time.

form Physical condition or fitness.

fractures Breaks or cracks in the bone.

heptathlon A two-day athletics competition that includes seven different disciplines: the 100 metres hurdles, high jump, shot put, 200 metres, long jump, javelin and 800 metres.

invincible Unbeatable.

javelin An athletics event in which participants compete to throw a long pointed spear, called a javelin, the furthest distance.

media Ways of communicating, for example through TV, radio, newspapers or websites.

overawed Intimidated by how impressive someone or something is.

pentathlon A five-event competition involving running, swimming, shooting, fencing and riding.

personal best The highest score or fastest time an athlete achieves in his or her career.

physiotherapist A health professional who works with people to improve their ability to move.

plyometrics A type of training that focuses on improving muscle power by stretching and contracting muscles.

psychology The study of the human mind and how it works.

role model Someone who is successful in sport or some other field. The way they behave is often copied by others, especially young people.

shot put An athletics event in which participants compete to throw a heavy metal ball, or 'shot', the furthest distance.

soft-tissue therapist A health professional who works with people to repair injuries and improve the function of soft-tissue, such as muscles and tendons, in the body.

sponsors Companies that pay money to someone in return for advertising their products, for example by wearing clothing with a company's logo.

unfounded Having no basis in fact.

Index

INSPIRATIONAL LIVES

Contents of new titles in the series

Tom Daley
978 0 7502 7999 4

Diving superstar
Taking the plunge
Conquering fears
Beating the adults
Early setbacks
Back on top
First Olympics
World beater
Darkest days
London looms
Olympic hero
A day in the life of Tom Daley
The impact of Tom Daley
Have you got what it takes
  to be a world-beating diver?

Jessica Ennis
978 0 7502 7998 7

The world's greatest all-rounder
Early potential
A growing medal collection
Senior breakthrough
Injury nightmare
On top of the world
A winning habit
Joy turns to anxiety
Back on track
Golden girl
Honouring a champion
A day in the life of Jessica Ennis
The impact of Jessica Ennis
Have you got what it takes
  to be an Olympic champion?

Mo Farah
978 0 7502 7996 3

Mighty Mo
Growing up in Africa
A new start
Schoolboy champion
Learning his craft
Time to get serious
Tough at the top
Getting faster
On top of the world
Olympic hero
Time to celebrate
A day in the life of Mo Farah
The impact of Mo Farah
Have you got what it takes
  to be a champion runner?

Ellie Simmonds
978 0 7502 7800 3

Paralympic glory
Small, that's all
Into the pool
Making sacrifices
In competition
Ellie's first Paralympics
Dealing with fame
In training
Building on Beijing
A day in the life of Ellie Simmonds
Second time around
After the Games
The impact of Ellie Simmonds
Have you got what it takes
  to be a champion swimmer?

WAYLAND